D0455330

THE COMPLETE BEATLES QUIZ BOOK

THE COMPLETE
BEATLES

QUIZ BOOK

Bell Publishing Company
New York

Copyright © 1975 by Edwin Goodgold and Dan Carlinsky
All rights reserved.

This 1982 edition is published by Bell Publishing Company,
distributed by Crown Publishers, Inc. by arrangement with
Carlinsky & Carlinsky, Inc. and Edwin Goodgold.

Library of Congress Cataloging in Publication Data

Goodgold, Edwin.
   The complete Beatles quiz book.

   1. Beatles—Miscellanea.   2. Rock musicians—
England—Biography.   I. Carlinsky, Dan.
II. Title.
ML421.B4G66   1982   784.5'4'00922   82-4571
                                        AACR2

ISBN: 0-517-387700

h g f e d c b a

with special thanks to
John, Paul, George, Ringo, and Jules Solobkowicz

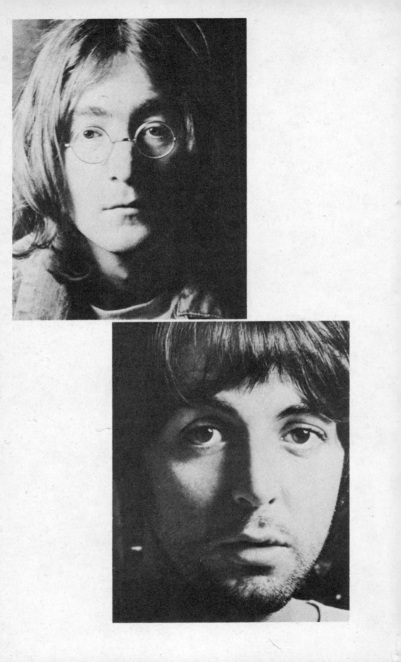

Acknowledgments

Thanks to: Nancy Carlinsky, Susan Moldow, Henry Gross; Malcolm C. Brown, Tony King, and L. G. Wood of EMI Records Ltd.; the gang at SAS; Bob Abel and Leonore Fleischer.

Photos on pages 50 and 114, taken in Hamburg, Germany, in 1961, are available from Jurgen Vollmer, Box 165, Brooklyn, N.Y. 11202.

Introduction

The Beatles need no introduction.

According to the Lyrics . . .

Questions culled from all manner of Beatle songs.

1. What's Maxwell's last name and what was he majoring in?

2. Would the Beatles believe in a love at first sight?

3. Name the song in which the Beatles sing:
   Falling, yes I am falling,
   And she keeps calling
   Me back again.

4. According to EVERY LITTLE THING, what do I remember about the first time?

5. Which airline do the Beatles patronize in their trip from Miami back to the U.S.S.R.?

6. According to the lyric of A DAY IN THE LIFE, what did the man in the news do to merit attention?

7. The Beatles sing: *Close your eyes and I'll kiss you.* What will happen tomorrow?

8. In REVOLUTION, what can you do when you talk about destruction, as far as the Beatles are concerned?

9. Why don't the Beatles *care too much for money?*

10. What must I do before I tell HER MAJESTY I love her a lot?

11. Who can succeed like Dr. Robert?

12. DON'T LET ME DOWN describes a love that lasts forever. What do we know about that love's history?

13. Where does ELEANOR RIGBY keep the face she wears?

    A. *in a car by the moor*
    B. *in a jar by the door*
    C. *in a bar serving Coors*
    D. *in Mackenzie's desk drawer*

14. In HERE, THERE AND EVERYWHERE, how easily can the Beatles' girl change their life?

15. What does the little girl in I FEEL FINE tell all the world?

16. What kind of winter do the Beatles survive in HERE COMES THE SUN? Give three adjectives, please.

17. Where did all the Beatles' troubles seem to be YESTERDAY?

18. In A HARD DAY'S NIGHT, what do the Beatles know will happen to them when they get you alone?

19. And when they do, how do the things that you do make them feel?

20. In SHE SAID, SHE SAID, how does she make the Beatles feel?

21. Because life is very short, what don't the Beatles have time for, my friend?

    A. out-of-tune sitars
    B. wasting their love
    C. fussing and fighting
    D. reading books like this

22. What does the Beatles' GIRL do when friends are there?

23. In DAY TRIPPER, what kind of engagements does the Beatles' girl play exclusively?

24. I'LL FOLLOW THE SUN. But why?

25. What will happen if you say THE WORD the Beatles are thinking of? (If you answer that a duck will come down and give you $100, you're wrong.)

Girls

The Liverpool lads have sung the praises of more than one female—a chapter's worth, in fact.

1. Who *picks up the rice in the church where a wedding has been?*
2. MEAN MR. MUSTARD'S sister.
3. Who was the lovely student who had her skull bashed in by Maxwell's shiny smasher?

    A. Rita
    B. Lucy
    C. Joan
    D. Vera
    E. Jennifer
    F. Andrea

4. Who chanted *"Maxwell Must Go Free!"* from the gallery?

5. On the "Let It Be" album, *the judge he guilty found her.* Who's "her"?

6. *Her name was Magill, and she called herself Lil, but everyone knew her as* _____.

7. Who speaks *words of wisdom*?

8. In WHEN I'M SIXTY-FOUR, sister of Chuck and Dave.

9. Who climbs the Eiffel Tower in I AM THE WALRUS?

    A. The Eggman's wife

    B. Mrs. Walrus

    C. Semolina Pilchard

    D. Farina McKenzie

    E. Harriett Chaff

    F. Aunt Ruth

10. What early girlfriend of song do the Beatles set free to go with another guy?

11. Whom do the Beatles threaten: *Oooh, you'll get yours yet?*

12. Which young lady performed the Stroll in such fashion as to make the Beatles dizzy?

13. Who has *seashell eyes*?

14. *When you find yourself in the thick of it, help yourself to a bit of what is all around you, Silly Girl.* Who receives this sage advice from the Beatles?

15. Whom do the Beatles tell to *greet the brand new day-hay-hay-hay* and *see the sunny sky-hi-hi-hies?*

14

Rhyming Lyrics

It might be fun to take some time
And finish up each Beatle rhyme.
Now if you get them all, my dear,
There'll be no doubt—you're fab and gear.

1. *Help me if you can, I'm feeling down . . .*
2. *You're asking me, will my love grow? . . .*
3. *I want you so bad . . .*
4. *Although I laugh and I act like a clown . . .*
5. *I'M LOOKING THROUGH YOU*
   Where did you go? . . .
6. *HOLD ME TIGHT,*
   Tell me I'm the only one . . .
7. *She feels good, she knows she's looking fine . . .*
8. *Open up your eyes now,*
   TELL ME WHAT YOU SEE . . .
9. *I wouldn't let you leave me 'cause it's true . . .*
10. *Time after time you refuse to even listen . . .*

"You've Got to Hide Your Love Away": Hidden Song Titles

Play Beatlesleuth and ferret out the song titles buried in these ridiculous sentences. Ignore punctuation, spacing and, of course, meaning. Example: DO YOU HAVE T*HE LP* I GAVE YOU?

1. PERUVIAN PIED PIPER: "WHEN I FIFE, LLAMAS COME RUNNING."

2. JOHN'S A REAL COMIC. HELL, EVEN PAUL SAYS SO.

3. WERE THEY JUDEO-CHRISTIAN ETHICS OR HINDU MORES?

4. IF YOU MAKE THE MAHARISHI AN OMELET IT BETTER NOT BE A WESTERN.

5. ORIENTAL WOODSMAN'S PROVERB: "SHARP AX, ONE CHOP; BLUNT AX, MANY CHOPS."

"Yesterday": The Early Years

The Beatles, of course, were doing their thing long before their name became a household word. Here are ten questions to test the student of early Beatlehistory.

1. Explain the chant: "Ringo never, Pete forever!"

2. Put into chronological order: Moondogs, Silver Beatles, Quarrymen.

3. "The Mecca of Beat" describes which Liverpool club?
    A. The Tavern
    B. The Cavern
    C. The Canyon
    D. The Limehouse

4. Who were the Nurk twins?

5. Who was Stu Sutcliffe and what became of him?

6. Which major record company rejected the Beatles?

7. True or false: Ringo got his job with the Beatles by answering an ad in *Mersey Beat,* the Liverpool music paper.

8. Where are The Top Ten Club, The Star Club, and The Kaiserkeller?

9. For whom did the Beatles serve as backup band in their first professional recording?

10. It was the Beatles' recording of _____ that brought them to the attention of Brian Epstein.

John

1. John studied at:
    A. Liverpool College of Music
    B. Liverpool College of Art
    C. Liverpool A&M
    D. Oxford University
    E. Villanova
2. John's father's first name, please.
3. Who raised John?
4. What was his middle name before he switched it to Ono?
5. Who is Julian?
6. Name John's brother.
7. Which of the following books were not written by John:
    A. *A Spaniard in the Works*

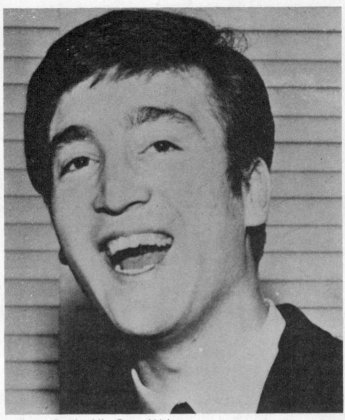

B. *In His Own Write*

C. *A Spaniard Can Write*

8. True or false: Cynthia Powell was John's second wife.

9. True or false: John named his cat Jesus.

10. In which of these songs does John sing lead:

    A. YES IT IS

    B. SHE SAID, SHE SAID

    C. NO REPLY

    D. ANYTIME AT ALL

    E. I SHOULD HAVE KNOWN BETTER

Paul

1. Francie Schwartz and Ronnie Spector were both Paul's
    A. backup vocalists
    B. high school teachers
    C. girlfriends
    D. dancing instructors

2. True or false: Paul and Linda staged a "Bed-In" for peace during their honeymoon.

3. Give the name of Paul's beloved sheepdog.

4. Who is Mike McGear?

5. True or false: Paul was the one who went to court to dissolve the Beatles.

6. Besides Linda, what lucky lady was engaged to marry Paul?

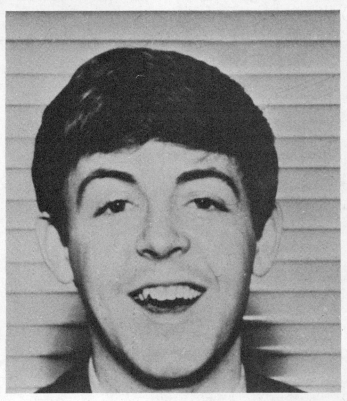

7. On what continent was Paul's album "Band on the Run" recorded?

8. What is the significance of the address Kintyre, Argyllshire, Scotland?

9. What is Paul's middle name?

10. In which of these songs does Paul sing lead:

    A. LADY MADONNA

    B. ANOTHER GIRL

    C. I'VE JUST SEEN A FACE

    D. YOU WON'T SEE ME

    E. WHEN I'M SIXTY-FOUR

George

1. What's George's favorite candy?
2. True or false: George named BLUE JAY WAY after a house he had rented in Hollywood.
3. How does George's guitar weep?
4. Who instructed him in the fine art of sitar playing?
5. Name George's parents.
6. What is an Apple scruff?
7. What color are George's eyes?
8. Who are Peter and Harry?
9. True or false: On the cover of a solo album George is quoted as saying, "I don't believe in the Beatles."
10. In which of these songs does George sing lead:

    A. ROLL OVER BEETHOVEN
    B. DON'T BOTHER ME
    C. IF I NEEDED SOMEONE
    D. TAXMAN
    E. WHILE MY GUITAR GENTLY WEEPS

Ringo

1. What is Ringo's real name?
2. What's Dingle?
3. True or false: Ringo once was drummer for Rory Storme and the Hurricanes.
4. In what year did Ringo become a Beatle?
5. Who are Zak and Jason?
6. What was Ringo's famous reply to the question, "What do you think of Beethoven?"
7. And why did he say he wore so many rings on his fingers?
8. What did Ringo have removed in an operation in December, 1964?
9. True or false: Ringo is naturally blond.
10. In which of these songs does Ringo sing lead:
    A. GOOD DAY SUNSHINE
    B. I WANT TO HOLD YOUR HAND
    C. I CALL YOUR NAME
    D. SOMETHING
    E. MICHELLE

"I've Just Seen a Face":
Place the Eyes and Noses

Pictured here are four pairs of Beatleyes. Can you tell who owns each set?

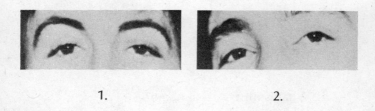

1.   2.

3.   4.

Now do the same with these Beatlenoses.

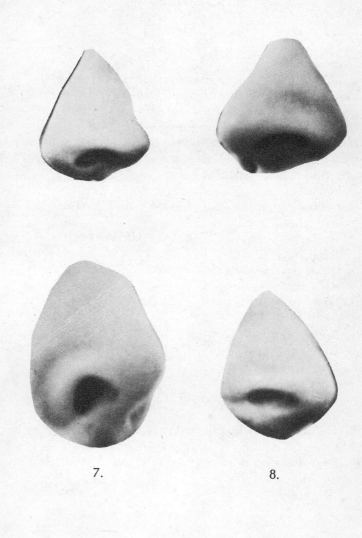

7.

8.

Silly Syllables

Not all Beatlelyrics are words that can be found in your friendly neighborhood dictionary. In backgrounds (and occasionally foregrounds) here and there in the Beatle literature, you'll find various oohs, aahs and la-de-dahs. If you really know the songs below, you'll be able to match them with the appropriate silly syllables.

1. Beep-beep, mm-beep-beep
2. He-la, he-ba, hel-lo-a (cha cha)
3. Da da da, da-da da da, da-da da da
4. Tu-tu-tu-tu tu-tu-tu-tu tu-tu-tu-tu
5. Bom-pa bom
6. Da-da daa da-da dun dun daa, da-da daa da-da dun dun daa
7. Bop shoo-op mm-bop bop shoo-op
8. Sha la la la la la la-ah
9. Goo goo g'joob
10. Doo-doo doo-doo doo doo

FROM ME TO YOU

I AM THE WALRUS

BABY IT'S YOU

HELLO, GOODBYE

HEY JUDE

DRIVE MY CAR

BOYS

ALL TOGETHER NOW
GIRL
HAPPINESS IS A WARM GUN

THE BEATLES BY ROYAL COMMAND

(Extra credit) OB-LA-DI, OB-LA-DA tells the saga of
    A. Esmond and Polly Jones
    B. Desmond and Polly Jones
    C. Molly and Esmond Jones
    D. Desmond and Molly Jones
    E. Jeremy and Liza Eschelbacher

Flip Sides

First, match the song with its opposite number.

1. HELP   RAIN
2. TICKET TO RIDE   YES IT IS
3. PAPERBACK WRITER   I'M DOWN
4. GET BACK   THINGUMYBOB
5. YELLOW SUBMARINE   DON'T LET ME DOWN

Now, with no hints at all, tell what's on the flip side of these.

   6. LET IT BE
   7. HELLO, GOODBYE
   8. I WANT TO HOLD YOUR HAND
   9. WE CAN WORK IT OUT
  10. HEY JUDE

Faraway Places
(And Some Close Ones, Too)

These questions ask about places mentioned here and there in the Beatles' musical travels.

1. According to BACK IN THE U.S.S.R., girls who *really knock me out* come from _____ and girls who *make me sing and shout* come from _____.

2. According to THE BALLAD OF JOHN AND YOKO, when the happy couple were standing at the dock at Southampton where were they trying to go?

3. Later, they honeymooned near what river?

4. Where is PENNY LANE, according to the song?

5. Where does *the celebrated Mr. K* perform?

6. Where does ROCKY RACCOON live?

7. Where was HONEY PIE employed before she went to Hollywood and became a movie star?

8. Where does THE LONG AND WINDING ROAD lead?

9. In WHEN I'M SIXTY-FOUR, where do the Beatles suggest renting a cottage, *if it's not too dear?*

10. On "*Magical Mystery Tour*" the Beatles find themselves in
    A. Peacock Alley
    B. Strawberry Fields
    C. Penny Lane
    D. Blue Jay Way
    E. Wales

11. Where is there nothing real and *nothing to get hung about?*
    A. Blue Jay Way
    B. Apple Alley, Liverpool
    C. Cheyenne, Wyoming
    D. Back in the U.S.S.R.
    E. Strawberry Fields

12. Where's the place the Beatles can go when they feel low and blue?

13. Where was Jo-Jo domiciled? Which state's grass does he favor?

14. And to where is he told to return?

15. Where does the NOWHERE MAN live?

What Do You Know?

A test based on Beatlelyrics.

1. What does THE FOOL ON THE HILL see?

2. In YOU WON'T SEE ME, what do the Beatles predict will occur if their girl won't see them?

3. *Come on back and see*
   Just what you mean to me
   is a supplication made in _____.

4. Where does Baby in BABY YOU'RE A RICH MAN keep all his money?
   - A. in a big brown bag
   - B. under my love mattress, babe
   - C. next to my heart
   - D. in the Liverpool Saving & Loan
   - E. in tax-free municipal bonds

5. Which song talks about *times of trouble*?

6. According to the song HELP!, in how many ways did the Beatles' life change?

7. Which day of the week is omitted in LADY MADONNA?

8. In YOU LIKE ME TOO MUCH, what will happen if you leave me?

9. Complete the analogy: Yes:No::Stop:Go:: Goodbye:Hello::High:Low::Why:_____.

10. What did John and Yoko eat in Vienna? (Hint: They ate it in a bag.)

    A. Vienna sausages

    B. popcorn (without butter)

    C. rolled oats, honey, and wheat germ

    D. rolled oats, honey, and sunflower seeds

    E. chocolate cake

11. If you don't take her out tonight, what will happen to your relationship with that girl?

12. Is MAGGIE MAE clean or dirty?

13. What photographs are displayed in the barber's shop on PENNY LANE?

14. What's the first thing a smart girl should do, according to the lyric of IF I NEEDED SOMEONE, if she'd like to hear from the Beatles?

15. What book did ROCKY RACCOON find in his room when he checked in?

16. Why do I think I'm going to be sad today?

    A. *My baby's old-fashioned momma's come to stay.*

    B. *The girl that's driving me mad is going away.*

    C. *The guru told me I should start to pray.*

    D. *My blind date's hair is curly, thin and gray.*

17. When the Beatles insist, TELL ME WHY, what are they trying to find out?

18. SHE'S LEAVING HOME, eh? At what time?

19. In YOU CAN'T DO THAT, what is it you can't do?

20. Complete the psychedelic image by matching the following, from LUCY IN THE SKY WITH DIAMONDS:

plasticene	trees
marshmallow	skies
looking glass	flowers
cellophane	pies
marmalade	taxis
newspaper	porters
tangerine	ties

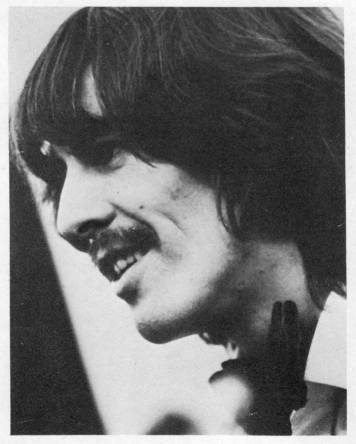

Which Came First?

Test your knowledge of Beatletime. You don't have to recall exact dates—you just need a good sense of relativity. Which came first?

1. "Beatles VI" or "Beatles '65"?
2. George or Paul? (Who joined the group first?)
3. The Beatles and LSD or the Beatles and the Maharishi?
4. The album, "A Hard Day's Night" or the album, "Something New"?
5. Ringo or John? (Who's older?)
6. HELLO, GOODBYE or NOWHERE MAN?
7. *Help!* or *Magical Mystery Tour*?
8. "The Beatles are more popular than Jesus" or the "death" of Paul?
9. STRAWBERRY FIELDS or PENNY LANE?
10. John's marriage to Cynthia or Ringo's marriage to Maureen?
11. HEY JUDE or LADY MADONNA?
12. *I get high with a little help from my friends* or *I get by with a little help from my friends*?

Numerology

Everything here has to do with numbers or mathematics, but you don't have to be a mathematician to score well. In fact, you hardly have to know how to add. Just remember what the Beatles taught you.

1. How old was the girl the Beatles danced with (you know, the one whose looks were way beyond compare)?

2. In AND YOUR BIRD CAN SING, how many wonders does the Beatles' cocky friend claim to have seen?

3. In YOU CAN'T DO THAT, how many times did the Beatles catch their girl talking with another man?

4. How often ain't the Beatles got nothing but love?

5. Complete: 1, 2, 3, 4, 5, 6, 7. . . .

6. According to BEING FOR THE BENEFIT OF MR. KITE, how many somersaults will Mr. H undertake on solid ground tonight?

7. How long is the PAPERBACK WRITER's *magnum opus*?

8. According to the news, how many holes were there in Blackburn, Lancashire?

9. She said she'd always been a dancer, she worked at _____ clubs a day.

10. What arithmetic lesson is taught by the Beatles in COME TOGETHER?

Analogies

And now on to higher math and logic. Fill in the blanks correctly to complete the analogies.

1. Boston:Bostonian::Liverpool: _____.

2. I WANT YOU (SHE'S SO HEAVY):Yoko::SEXY SADIE: _____.

3. I FEEL FINE:SHE'S A WOMAN::SOMETHING: _____.

4. Dr. Frankenstein:Igor::Prof. Foot: _____.

5. Northern Songs Ltd.:John and Paul:: _____:George.

6. I'M A LOSER:"Beatles '65"::IF I FELL: _____.

7. THINK FOR YOURSELF:George::THAT WOULD BE SOMETHING: _____.

8. "The Beatles" ("The White Album"):Apple:: _____:Capitol.

9. *How does it feel to be one of the beautiful people?*:BABY YOU'RE A RICH MAN::*All the lonely people, where do they all come from?*: _____.

10. The Muffin Man:Drury Lane::the barber: _____.

"I Saw a Film Today, Oh Boy":
Beatle Movies

The Beatles had more success on film than any other rock group. They left us a celluloid legacy rich in humor, adventure, and music. Also a bundle of memories that make great material for a quiz like this.

1. Which is the correct title:
   A. *A Hard Day's Night*
   B. *Hard Day's Night*
   C. *A Hard Days' Night*
   D. *Hard Days' Night*
   E. *A Hard Day Is Knight*
2. Name the warring factions in *Yellow Submarine*.
3. Where was *Help!* filmed?
4. In which movie does John say "I want to thank you on behalf of the group and I hope we passed the audition?"
5. A stuffed shirt on the train in *A Hard Day's Night* complains about the Beatles' loud transistor radio: "I fought the war for your sort." What is John's snappy answer?
6. On the train, Paul's grandfather announces his:
   A. marriage
   B. divorce
   C. engagement
   D. confirmation
7. Who played the grandfather?

8. Name the high priest of the Kaili in *Help!*

9. What other British rock group appears in *Magical Mystery Tour*?

10. Who is Old Fred?

11. In *Help!*, who shrinks to roughly the size of a guitar pick?

12. What was the original title of *Help!*?

13. Name the eight seas through which the Yellow Submarine travels in the movie.

14. At the end of *Let It Be*, where do the Beatles perform al fresco?

15. What is the chief Blue Meanie called in *Yellow Submarine*?

16. In *Help!*, what piece of music soothes the fierce Tiger, Raja?

17. What book is Ringo shown reading in *A Hard Day's Night*?

18. In which movie does Jeremy Hilary Boob appear?

19. In *Help!*, how does John wake up his comrades?

20. What are the names of the Beatles' road manager and his assistant in *A Hard Day's Night*?

21. Who is Michael Lindsay-Hogg?

22. According to the credits, who stars in *Yellow Submarine*?

23. In *A Hard Day's Night*, Ringo places his coat over a series of water puddles (*a la* Sir Walter Raleigh) for a woman to step on. The fifth time, she disappears. Why?

24. In the underwear scene in *Help!*, Ringo wears:

      A. white-and-blue striped boxer shorts
      B. white BVD's
      C. flower print shorts
      D. no underwear at all

25. Match the Beatle with the correct extraBeatle activity—all movies:

A. Wonderwall	John
B. Candy	Paul
C. How I Won the War	George
D. The Family Way	Ringo

Multiple Choice

This quiz is designed to:
   A. test your Beatleknowledge
   B. start you singing
   C. make you laugh
   D. all of the above
Answer: D.

1. Sgt. Pepper taught the band to play
   A. *yesterday*
   B. *20 years ago today*
   C. *October 17, 1963*
   D. *on Guy Fawkes Day*
2. When the doctor came to see ROCKY RAC-COON, what had the doc been drinking?
   A. piña colada
   B. Cel-Ray Tonic
   C. Orange Julius
   D. a vodka martini
   E. gin
3. Henry the Horse dances
   A. the Stroll
   B. the Funky Chicken
   C. the tango
   D. the waltz
4. How nice a girl is HER MAJESTY?
   A. damned nice
   B. not very nice at all
   C. nyeh!
   D. pretty nice

5. In NORWEGIAN WOOD, where do the Beatles crawl off to sleep?

    A. on a Castro convertible

    B. on a pile of straw

    C. in a bath

    D. in a Holiday Inn

    E. in Rocky Raccoon's den

6. In RUN FOR YOUR LIFE, the Beatles would rather see their *little girl* dead than

    A. red

    B. with a roadie

    C. with Pete Best

    D. with another man

7. Of all the Beatles' friends and lovers, according to the words of IN MY LIFE, no one compares with

    A. Eleanor Rigby

    B. Ringo

    C. you

    D. me

    E. Ethel

    F. Goodgold and Carlinsky

8. Which of the following songs does not appear on the album, "Let It Be?"

    A. ACROSS THE UNIVERSE

    B. THE LONG AND WINDING ROAD

    C. WE KNOW EACH OTHER

    D. I DIG A PONY

9. *What would you do if I sang out of tune? Would you . . .*

    A. *open the door and bark the cat?*

    B. *tell all your friends?*

    C. *stand up and walk out on me?*

    D. *stop buying my records?*

10. How big is the chip on the Beatles' shoulder in I'LL CRY INSTEAD?

    A. bigger than a breadbox

    B. bigger than an agent's heart

    C. smaller than their love for you, babe

    D. exactly as large as Ringo's nose

    E. bigger than their feet

11. Which of the following recorded at least one Lennon/McCartney tune?

    A. Patti Page

    B. Duke Ellington

    C. Peggy Lee

    D. the Boston Pops Orchestra

    E. the Maharishi Mahesh Yogi

12. Who is the featured vocalist with Sgt. Pepper's musicmakers?

    A. *the inimitable Ray Davies*

    B. *the incomparable Keith Moon*

    C. *the unbelievable Tony Bennett*

    D. *the one and only Billy Shears*

    E. *Sgt. Pepper himself (singing falsetto)*

    F. *Ian Dove and Bill Graham (what a duo!)*

"With a Little Help from My Friends": Borrowed Tunes

On rare occasions, particularly in the early days, the Beatles recorded songs they didn't write, giving them the special Beatle stamp. Do you know who wrote what?

1. Who wrote ROLL OVER BEETHOVEN and ROCK AND ROLL MUSIC?

2. Which song composed by Meredith Willson for *The Music Man* was recorded by the Beatles?

3. What Leiber-Stoller song recorded by the Beatles depicts a city where *I'm gonna get my baby one time*?

4. Ric Marlow and Bobby Scott wrote this movie theme recorded by the Beatles. Name it.

5. The Beatles recorded two songs by Carl Perkins on one album. Name the tunes and the album.

6. Who did LONG TALL SALLY first?

7. What's the one Buddy Holly song the Beatles recorded?

8. The Beatles recut a hit made popular by Smokey Robinson and the Miracles. What was it?

9. What early Isley Brothers hit was re-recorded by the Beatles? (Hint: *Shake it up, baby!*)

10. BAD BOY and SLOW DOWN were both composed by _____.

True or False

Either it's true or it's false—it can't be both. You decide.

1. Paul plays lefthanded. True or false?
2. The original HEY JUDE single is more than seven minutes long. True or false?
3. The Beatles once toured with Elvis. True or false.
4. WITHIN YOU WITHOUT YOU begins with sitar music. True or false?
5. The Beatles sang TILL THERE WAS YOU on the Ed Sullivan TV show. True or false?
6. Ringo's starting salary as a Beatle was £25 a week. True or false?
7. Brian Epstein once was a record retailer in Liverpool. True or false?
8. Boob traveled economy class aboard the Yellow Submarine. True or false?
9. Ringo led the Liverpool Little Cricket League in batting two years in a row. True or false?
10. John and Yoko have made a 60-minute film that consists solely of John smiling. True or false?

Anatomy of the Beatles:
Eyes, Arms, Lips, Etc.

The Beatles, in their songs, often describe parts of the body in unusual, picturesque terms—terms that should stick in your memory.

1. What kind of arms and lips do the Beatles have? (FROM ME TO YOU)
2. Describe Lucy's eyes. (LUCY IN THE SKY WITH DIAMONDS)
   A. diamond-shaped
   B. cashew
   C. kaleidoscope
   D. hazel
   E. psychedelic
   F. astigmatic
3. In BLACKBIRD, what kind of wings are needed to learn to fly? What kind of eyes to see?
4. According to COME TOGETHER, how long is Flat Top's hair? What kind of finger does he have and what kind of eyeball?
5. MEAN MR. MUSTARD keeps a _____ up his nose.

Who Sang Lead?

Match the lead singer with the song.

1.
A. EVERY LITTLE THING   George
B. FOR YOU, BLUE   John
C. ACT NATURALLY   Ringo
2.
A. PAPERBACK WRITER   Ringo
B. RAIN   Paul
C. WHAT GOES ON   John
3.
A. BLUE JAY WAY   George
B. EIGHT DAYS A WEEK   Paul
C. THE NIGHT BEFORE   John
4.
A. BABY'S IN BLACK   John and Paul
B. I'LL FOLLOW THE SUN   George
C. CHAINS   Paul
5.
A. I FEEL FINE   George
B. SHE'S A WOMAN   John
C. THE INNER LIGHT   Paul

"Say the Word":
One-Word Answers

The answer to each of these questions is a single word. Go.

1. I DON'T WANT TO SPOIL THE PARTY. So what should I do?
2. Send her back to me
   'Cause everyone can see
   Without her I will be
   In _____.
3. Two colors are mentioned in BABY'S IN BLACK. One color you know about already. What's the other?
4. In AND I LOVE HER, how does she give everything to the Beatles?

5. In ACROSS THE UNIVERSE, what's gonna change the Beatles' world?

6. For whom isn't *that boy* (from THIS BOY) good?

7. With whom would the Beatles like to be in an OCTOPUS'S GARDEN?

8. What made it possible for the Beatles to hear bells, birds, and love?

9. What should you be when you discover that SHE LOVES YOU?

10. According to I CALL YOUR NAME, what can't I do at night?

    A. cry

    B. yodel

    C. sleep

    D. weep

11. Who in the world can do what the other girl in ANOTHER GIRL can do?

12. According to BECAUSE, what color is the sky?

"Do You Want to Know a Secret?":
Behind the Scenes

Unless you're a fan's fan, most of this chapter will leave you bamboozled. But read on—you might learn something.

1. Which Beatle was routinely the first dressed for performances?

2. What was Seltaeb?

3. Who is credited with thinking up the film title, *A Hard Day's Night*?

4. What does Erich ("Love Story") Segal have to do with the Beatles?

5. Match the man behind the scenes with the role he played.

A. second road manager   Derek Taylor
B. first road manager   Mal Evans
C. song publisher   Neil Aspinall
D. film director   Dick James
E. publicist   Brian Epstein
F. manager   Richard Lester

6. Who played organ on the album, "Let It Be?"

7. Is Northern Songs Ltd. or Unltd.?

8. Who, being 64 years old when the song was written, inspired WHEN I'M SIXTY-FOUR?

9. What did Billy J. Kramer with the Dakotas and Gerry and the Pacemakers have in common with the Beatles?

10. What is the London street address of Apple Records?

Jurgen Vollmer

Song Fragments

If you're good, you should be able to come up with the correct song title from even the skimpiest of clues—like these bits and pieces.

1. *sitting on a cornflake*
2. *velvet hand*
3. *her little white book*
4. *trampoline*
5. *pictures of Chairman Mao*
6. *a short haired girl who sometimes wears it twice as long*
7. *arrives without a suitcase*
8. *something I can blab about*
9. *by the banks of her own lagoon*
10. *life of ease*

(If you're having a tough time of it, here's an out-of-order list of the correct titles. Match them. LADY MADONNA, REVOLUTION, OLD BROWN SHOE, SHE CAME IN THROUGH THE BATHROOM WINDOW, GOOD DAY SUNSHINE, HAPPINESS IS A WARM GUN, LOVELY RITA, YELLOW SUBMARINE, I AM THE WALRUS, BEING FOR THE BENEFIT OF MR. KITE.)

Song Beginnings

Match the words or sounds with the song they begin.

1. If you want it here it is . . .
2. Love, love, love; love, love, love; love, love, love . . .
3. You'll never know how much I really love you, You'll never know how much I really care . . .
4. She's not a girl who misses much . . .
5. To lead a better life I need my love to be here . . .

6. Like a Rolling Stone! . . .
7. Come on, come on; come on, come on . . .
8. Once there was a way to get back homeward . . .
9. I told you 'bout Strawberry Fields, you know, the place where nothing is real . . .
10. (A rooster crowing.)

DO YOU WANT TO KNOW A SECRET?
HAPPINESS IS A WARM GUN

HERE, THERE AND EVERYWHERE

DIG IT
EVERYBODY'S GOT SOMETHING TO HIDE EXCEPT
ME AND MY MONKEY
COME AND GET IT
ALL YOU NEED IS LOVE
GOLDEN SLUMBERS
GOOD MORNING, GOOD MORNING

GLASS ONION

Song Endings

Now, match the *endings* to the songs.

1. . . . *My baby don't care.*
2. . . . *You-ou you-ou you—you-ou you-ou you—I love you.*
3. . . . (laughter)
4. . . . (grunting)
5. . . . *Believe me when I tell you I'll never do you no harm.*
6. . . . *I've got time, I've got time, I've got time.*
7. . . . *No no no, no no no, no no no, no no no. . . .*
8. . . . *La la la la la la.*
9. . . . *Yeah, yeah, yeah; yeah, yeah, yeah, yeah!*
10. . . . *Baby take a chance with me, oh yeah!*

RUN FOR YOUR LIFE
LITTLE CHILD

I WANT TO TELL YOU
TICKET TO RIDE
OH! DARLING

P.S. I LOVE YOU
SHE LOVES YOU

MISERY
OB-LA-DI, OB-LA-DA
PIGGIES

(Extra credit) What's the tail ending of A DAY IN THE
LIFE? (Hint: Neither words nor music.)

Name That Tune

The answer to every question in this section is a song title. That's all you need to know.

1. *Yeh, you got that something,*
   I think you'll understand,
   When I say that something,

   _____.

2. Complete: *Although she was born a long, long time ago. . . .*

3. Who threatens, *If you take a walk I'll tax your feet?*

4. Where does this line come from: *Say that I'm the only one and then I might never be the lonely one.*

5. *You're giving me the same old line,*
   I'm wondering why.
   You hurt me then
   You're back again.
   No, no, no,

   _____.

6. Which song speaks of negotiations, situation, and investigation?

7. I don't want to kiss you, hold your hand or do any of that stuff. What do I want to do?

8. *Tell me that you've got everything you want. . . .*

9. In which song do the Beatles plead, *It's so easy for a girl like you to lie—tell me why?*

10. *I'll be coming home again to you, love*
    And till the day I do, love

    _____.

11. How long will it be till I belong to you?
12. *Don't come around, leave me alone, _____.*
13. *Were you telling lies? and Was I so unwise?*
    were questions the Beatles asked about _____.
14. *Do what you want to do,*
    Go where you're going to,

    _____,

    'Cause I will be there with you.
15. *Someday when we're dreaming,*
    Deep in love, not a lot to say,
    Then we will remember

    _____.

AMERICA'S FINEST TEENAGE MAGAZINE

VALUABLE COLLECTOR'S EDITION ON

teen talk

THE BEATLES 35¢

MAY

Exclusive Photos - Intimate Secrets
FULL PAGES OF PICTURES SUITABLE FOR FRAMING

Beatle Grab Bag

A smorgasbord of Beatleana: help yourself. (Come back for seconds if you like.)

1. Which Beatle wears glasses in public?
2. What happened to the Beatles on June 12, 1965?
3. What is NORWEGIAN WOOD's subtitle?
4. Which Beatles song has been recorded more than any other?
5. Parlophone is the name of
   A. a telephone with a recessed mouthpiece
   B. a public affairs TV show in England hosted by John
   C. the record company that first signed the Beatles
   D. a telephone offtrack betting service, featured in *Magical Mystery Tour*
6. LOVE YOU TO features what Oriental instrument?
7. One song from the "Sgt. Pepper" album was banned by many radio stations on the grounds that it contained references to illegal drugs. Name the song and quote the taboo line.
8. At one memorable performance, John, ever the comic, announced, "The people in the cheap seats clap. The rest of you just rattle your jewelry." Who were "the rest of you"?
9. What do Mia Farrow, Mike Love (the

Beachgentleman), Donovan, and Mick Jagger have in common with the Beatles?

10. What unexpected musical ensemble is heard in ELEANOR RIGBY?

11. Why is the fire engine in PENNY LANE like Paul's grandfather in the movie *A Hard Day's Night*?

12. (And now for dessert.) Concoct the four proper delectable phrases from the ingredients mentioned in SAVOY TRUFFLE: sling, tangerine, coffee, creme, heart, ginger, pineapple, dessert.

What's Their Line?

Some people sing songs for a living. Some people write books. But there are characters in Beatlesongs who have funkier occupations. Do you remember?

1. What does LOVELY RITA do?
2. And Molly Jones?
3. What about the son of the dirty man in PAPERBACK WRITER?
4. What does the Walrus do on the side?
5. And what do the pretty nurses in PENNY LANE sell?

"Well Here's Another Clue for You": The "Death" of Paul

Just where, when, and why the stories began is a subject of some controversy, but what happened is clear: With no official fanfare, pronouncements, or hype, the word began to spread that Paul was dead. According to those who insisted they were in the know, clues were everywhere: on album covers, in personal appearances (or lack of them), in the music itself. Newspapers, magazines, and disc jockeys fueled the fire and legitimized the rumors that flew from fan to fan. The following are questions dealing with just a few highlights of this spooky period of Beatlehistory.

1. What is different about Paul's carnation inside the "Magical Mystery Tour" jacket?

2. In the fade of STRAWBERRY FIELDS, what some listeners think sounds like *I'm very bored* has been interpreted by others as _____ _____ _____.

3. A famous publicity still from the movie *Help!* showed all four Beatles tied together with a python-like ski scarf. Why was this picture interpreted as a hint of Paul's forthcoming demise?

4. Which song, if played backwards, supposedly reproduces the sounds of Paul's "fatal car accident"?

    A. REVOLUTION
    B. REVOLUTION #1
    C. REVOLUTION #9

5. What did adherents of the "Paul Is Dead" theory make of the yellow flower arrangement in the lower righthand corner of the "Sgt. Pepper" album cover?

6. What was the symbolism of the license plate on the white Volkswagen shown on the "Abbey Road" cover?

7. The accepted interpretation of the "Abbey Road" cover was that the walking Beatles formed a funeral procession. Paul, in bare feet and carrying a cancer stick in his right hand, is clearly the buryee. Judging by John's outfit, what was his role?

8. What was Ringo's role?

9. And what was George's role?

10. How did know-it-alls explain the fact that even after Paul's alleged demise four Beatles were still often seen and photographed?

Complete the Lyric

This quiz tests your fluency in the Beatle literature. In each case, simply supply the missing words.

1. *Roll up to the MAGICAL MYSTERY TOUR . . .*
2. *Lend me your ears and I'll sing you a song . . .*
3. *A, B, C, D . . .*
4. *E, F, G, H, I, J . . .*
5. *LOVE ME DO,*
   You know I love you,
   I'll always be true . . .
6. *Baby you can DRIVE MY CAR,*
   Guess I'm gonna be a star,
   Baby you can drive my car . . .
7. According to BECAUSE: *Love is all . . .*
8. *Words are flowing out like endless rain into a paper cup . . .*
9. *I got every reason on earth to be mad . . .*
10. *Please don't spoil my day*
    I'm miles away
    And after all . . .
11. *Me, I'm just the lucky kind . . .*
12. *I never weep at night . . .*
13. *If I'd been out till quarter to three . . .*
14. *And when I want to kiss you, yeah! All I've got to do is . . .*
15. *MICHELLE, ma belle . . .* (Complete in French; spelling counts.)

Hide and Seek

Buried away in this legion of letters are the names of 49 characters from Beatlesongs. You'll find them running from left to right, right to left, up to down, down to up, and diagonally. Circle them in the grid as you find them. Grab a pencil and start hunting.

```
E I Z Z I L S S I M A B E E T H O V E N
T B S C H U C K R E P P E P T G S L H R
H G I E L A R R E T L A W R I S E G O E
G Z B E I Z N E K C M R E H T A F C N D
I U M O L L Y M T Z H M A O N H K H I O
L K L Q D L L I G A M G I O U Y O K O M
N I L A E E L R U N V F R T V J U L I A
O A N N O D A M D N O M S E D G L F J T
O W M R P O S T M A N E J S P I I E K T
M R A R E V K S V L U A P A B F Y D L E
R T R Y T E G G M A N J M W W E J C D R
M O T H E R M A R Y U R O E X D K A U O
A L H O R I T A W N M L E R R C V O M L
X M A F B S L R I U A L K R A E L N N G
W B T T R P N O S G L J O N E S H M O N
E E Z W O W R T N E B B L Q Y B L W P I
L R N P W A A U H Y E C N E D U R P O K
L O F T N R B C X R C D M P Z Y C N A N
O P B S D C I L T E I D A S Y X E S Q U
E T I K R M O J O J B J N O A E D U J S
```

Now here's a second puzzle containing 41 song titles—all of them, of course, made famous by the Beatles. Pick up your pencil again.

```
X R E R D A E D Y L L A E R S I L U A P
C K C A B E B L L I N M Y L I F E F B Y
B O E C F K E B R M W T U K Y O B D A B
D M N Y S X O D E D I F I F E L L R I G
E M O M T Y R E K O L T I G I D S B N I
R G O E S H E S A W O M A N N A T I S R
I I N V N Z P A K N P S M O N E Y M D R
T B R I Q B L L Z T A R T T B L E E I O
O M O R L F M A E A I U H A F U S M A N
S I F D P P N F N H R A E S T V I I S A
M R W H R E B T I T E L W E W D T N E E
I D H J S J V D O O P B A C O G I E H L
M E A B U N U N E D P L L O O E S E S E
A I T S N G I L U T I A R N F I H D D D
L N G N K O R A I N R C U D U P L Y I U
O E O A I M W K H A T K S T S Y P O A J
S H E M N L E O U C Y B V I Z E R U S Y
E A S X G L Y W T U A I W M Z N T L E E
R N O A N W Z R H O D R X E Y O Y D H H
A D N T H G I N S Y A D D R A H A D S T
```

Mixed Beatles:
20 Questions From Everywhere

Some hard, some easy—but all tantalizing.

1. What do King Kong, Napoleon, the Boob, and Father McKenzie have in common?

2. The Maharishi Mahesh Yogi made his headquarters in the town of
   - A. Titipu
   - B. Hamburg
   - C. Rishikesh
   - D. Marrakech
   - E. Polykusch

3. What does ABK in ABKCO stand for?

4. "Two Virgins" is the name of
   - A. John and Yoko's first album
   - B. Paul and Linda's second album
   - C. George and Pattie's third album
   - D. Ringo's first two albums

5. In the beginning, what was the total number of strings regularly played by John, Paul, and George?

6. What's unusual about the composer credits of FLYING?

7. The Beatles' record producer was
   A. George Perry
   B. Brian Epstein
   C. Duke Snider
   D. George Martin
   E. Rink Babka

8. What did the Beatles dedicate "to Mr. Elias Howe, who in 1846 invented the sewing machine?"

9. Which early Beatlehit is quoted in the fade of ALL YOU NEED IS LOVE?

10. Recite the lyrics to WILD HONEY PIE—all of them.

11. What instrument does George play on NOR-WEGIAN WOOD?

12. What's the title of the Beatles' second album for Capitol?

Information, Please

If you used to sing along you'll have no trouble with these.

1. After you've worked all night like a dog, what should you be doing when you get home?

2. With what choice words do the Beatles ask for more love in I SHOULD HAVE KNOWN BETTER?

3. What words did the Beatles say last night to their girl?

4. In OLD BROWN SHOE, the Beatles are in a queue. What are they waiting for?
   A. the early edition of the London *Times*
   B. a bus to Penny Lane
   C. some more of your charms
   D. their dreamboat
   E. your sweet top lip

5. Who is the *stupid get* cursed by the Beatles in I'M SO TIRED?

6. In IT'S ONLY LOVE, what happens to the Beatles when they see you go by (my, oh my)?
   A. They get high.
   B. They sigh.
   C. They feel like they could fly.
   D. They count, *eins, zwei, drei.*

7. *They slip into the shade and sip their* _____.

8. What will happen *before this dance is through*?

9. According to AND I LOVE HER, what can never die?

MEET THE BEATLES!

The First Album by England's Phenomenal Pop Combo

10. How long have the Beatles known the delicate piece of information referred to in DO YOU WANT TO KNOW A SECRET?

11. If *it really doesn't matter if I'm wrong or right,* what song on the "Sgt. Pepper" album am I listening to?

12. If YOU KNOW MY NAME, what should you do?

13. How many kids are running in the yard of Desmond and Molly Jones?

     A. two
     B. one
     C. a couple
     D. a few
     E. too many

14. Identify the Beatletune from these two lines:
    If you need somebody to love
    Just look into my eyes.

15. What protected her when SHE CAME IN THROUGH THE BATHROOM WINDOW?

16. Why do the Beatles ask the LITTLE CHILD to take a chance and dance with them?

17. Who was *born a poor young country boy?*
    A. Ringo
    B. Mr. H
    C. Sgt. Pepper
    D. Mother Nature's son
    E. all of the above

18. Whom do the Beatles ask to *D-liver D-letter, D-sooner D-better?*

19. In I'LL GET YOU, how often have the Beatles imagined themselves in love with you?

20. *Her eyes they tantalize,*
    Her lips they thrill me . . .
        . . . and what about her heart?

21. Who's got the Beatles locked up in CHAINS?

22. According to DRIVE MY CAR, what *is all very fine?*

23. What do the Beatles ask Bungalow Bill?

24. Who or what *was waiting just for you* in SEXY SADIE?

25. In GLASS ONION, who is described as *trying to make ends meet?*
    A. Her Majesty
    B. Lady Madonna
    C. Penny Lane
    D. Sadie Hawkins
    E. Honeybee
    F. the Chancellor of the Exchequer

Multiple Choice Revisited

More nonsense.

1. An OCTOPUS'S GARDEN is
   A. in Hamburg, Germany
   B. under the sea
   C. across the street
   D. over the river and through the woods
2. Where did John and Yoko honeymoon in Amsterdam, according to their ballad?
   A. The Sheraton
   B. The Hilton
   C. Howard Johnson's Motor Lodge
   D. The Häagen-Dazs Inn
   E. The Ramada Onderzeeër
3. In LOVE ME DO, what kind of girl do the Beatles want to love?
   A. somebody old, someone new
   B. somebody borrowed, someone blue
   C. somebody new, someone like you
   D. somebody in chains, someone untrue
4. In GET BACK, Sweet Loretta Modern thought she was a woman but she was
   A. the Walrus
   B. another man
   C. not
   D. Sweet Georgia Brown
   E. Her Majesty's lady in waiting

5. What kind of screen is mentioned in HONEY PIE?

      A. insectproof

      B. the windscreen of my heart

      C. velvet

      D. silver

6. Complete the lyric: *I am he as you are he as. . . .*

      A. *. . . Tom is Jerry and Simon is Garfunkel.*

      B. *. . . He is he and she is he and it is he and we are he and they are he and everyone is he.*

      C. *. . . You are there and there you are.*

      D. *. . . You are me and we are all together.*

      E. *. . . Who's on first?*

7. *If you're down he'll pick you up* refers to

      A. Dr. Robert

      B. Dr. Pepper

      C. Dr. Scholl

      D. Billy Shears

      E. Mr. Kite

8. How small do the Beatles feel in YOU'VE GOT TO HIDE YOUR LOVE AWAY?
   A. *two foot small*
   B. *so small no one would love me*
   C. *as small as Rocky Raccoon*
   D. *trivial*

9. In GOT TO GET YOU INTO MY LIFE, how frequently do the Beatles need you?
   A. eight days a week
   B. more than you'll ever know
   C. every single day of their life
   D. every hour of their day
   E. on alternate Sundays from 2 to 5 in the afternoon

10. Why does the world turn the Beatles on?
    A. because it's round
    B. because of all the beautiful people
    C. because it's so pretty
    D. just because

11. In GOOD DAY SUNSHINE, what kind of tree do the Beatles and their girl lie beneath?
    A. an acacia
    B. a spreading chestnut
    C. a shady tree
    D. a bloomin' buttonwood
    E. a wuntoo

12. In 1964 a Detroit group of Beatlehaters formed a protest movement to drive the Beatles from our shores. Their slogan was:
    A. "More Motown, Less Liverpool"
    B. "Stamp Out the Beatles"
    C. "A Curse on the Beatles"
    D. "Buy American, Lick the Limeys"
    E. "WIN"

"With Love from Me to You": Identify the Autographs

Four of these autographs are authentic; the others are fakes. Can you spot the real signatures of John, Paul, George and Ringo?

1.

[signature: John Lennon]

A.

[signature: John Le...]

B.

[signature: John Lennon]

C.

2.

A.

B.

C.

3.

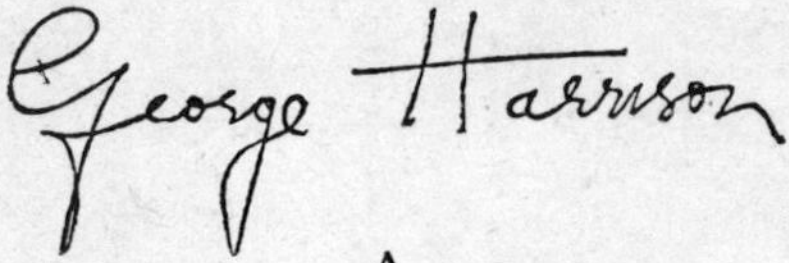

George Harrison

A.

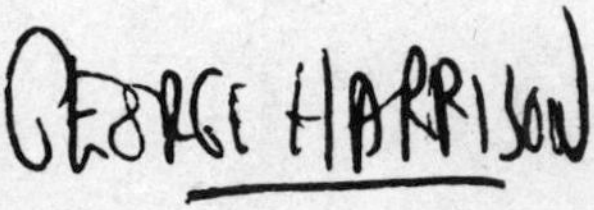

GEORGE HARRISON

B.

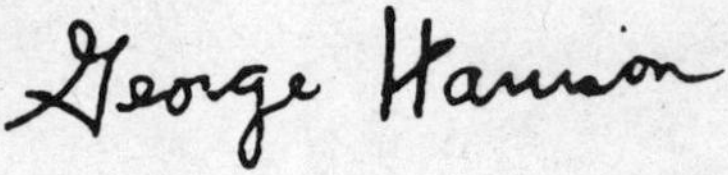

George Harrison

C.

4.

Ringo Starr

A.

Ringo Starr

B.

Ringo Starr

C.

The Amaze-ing Beatles

Grab a pencil and get set for a Magical Mystery Tour through this Beatle maze. Clue: Travel first to the chief Beatle, then to the Beatle nut, then to the quiet Beatle, and finally to the short Beatle before you find your way out of the apple. Time limit: 60 seconds.

From Liverpool

To Fame and Fortune

What's Missing? Fill in the Blanks

Careful when you complete these: some are tricky.

1. The Beatles have been in love before and they know that *love is more than* _____ _____ _____.

2. If you _____ _____ _____ I'LL BE BACK.

3. *Close your eyes and I'll kiss you,*
   Tomorrow I'll _____ _____.

4. *The minute you let her under your skin then you begin to* _____ _____ _____.

5. *Many times I've been alone and many times I've* _____.

6. According to WHILE MY GUITAR GENTLY WEEPS, we have been diverted, perverted, and _____.

7. *Jai guru deva* _____.

8. *We see the banker sitting waiting for a* _____.

9. *Turn off your mind, relax and* _____ _____.

10. _____ _____ darns *his socks in the night when there's nobody there.*

11. You may never give the Beatles your money but they, in return, never give you their _____.

12. ANOTHER GIRL will love the Beatles till _____ _____. (Hint: Not till the Twelfth of Never.)

13. The NOWHERE MAN resembles _____ _____ _____ a bit.

14. In WHEN I GET HOME, what don't the Beatles have time for?

Beatlecrostic

First, come up with the clue words and write them in the designated blanks. Next, transfer each letter that falls in a numbered blank to the proper box in the grid. When you've filled in the entire grid, you will behold a Beatle quotation of some significance. The first letters of the clue words, read from top to bottom, also make sense. Once you get going, you might find it profitable to work from grid to clue words as well as from clue words to grid.

Note: If you're going to share this book with a friend and don't want to give away the answers, or if you hate to write in your only copy, buy another one.

A. $\underline{L}\ \underline{o}\ \underline{v}\ \underline{E}$ Yesterday, this was such an easy
   4321
   game to play.

B. $\underline{}\ \underline{L}\ \underline{}\ \underline{}\ \underline{N}\ \underline{O}\ \underline{}$ Actress Bron in *Help!*
   $7257\ 60$

C. $\underline{}\ \underline{O}\ \underline{}\ \underline{}\ \underline{}\ \underline{E}\ \underline{}\ \underline{}\ \underline{S}\ \underline{O}\ \underline{N}\ \underline{G}\ \underline{S}$ Beatle
   27732258
   music publishing co.

D. $\underline{}\ \underline{O}\ \underline{}\ \underline{E}\ \underline{}\ \underline{L}\ \underline{}$ This happened once be-
   235030
   fore when I came to your door.

84

E. O C T O P U S , S   G A R D E N
   34   63   40 69
Hideaway beneath the waves.

F. B E M I Epstein agency.
   3 71

G. M A R Y   H O P K I N S Apple record-
   10   41   35   55 5
ing star ("Those Were the Days," etc.).

H. C A R R Y What you gotta do to that weight.
   54

I. _ _ _ I _ O _ Apple distributor.
        16 48

J. _ _ _ E S Your day breaks, your mind does
        13 68
this.

K. _ I C _ _ _ _ _ Help! director (given name).
   7 42

L. _ H _ O _ _   I T   _ W _ _
   2   64   47   66
Man buys ring, woman does this

M. N E V E R When you give me your money.
   17   45

N. _ _ E R _ _ T B   _ M R _
      36 52   74 46   20 37
Backed John on "Sometime in New York City"
album.

O. $\underline{Y}\ \underline{E}\ \underline{S}$ "_____ It Is."
     31

P. $\underline{H}\ \underline{E}\ \underline{L}\ \underline{P}$ $\underline{F}\ \underline{R}\ \underline{O}\ \underline{M}$ $\underline{M}\ \underline{Y}$
      78   65   49 11
   $\underline{F}\ \underline{R}\ \underline{I}\ \underline{E}\ \underline{N}\ \underline{D}\ \underline{S}$ A little of which allows me
     15   8
   to get by, etc.

Q. $\underline{A}$ $\underline{W}\ \underline{I}\ \underline{N}\ \underline{D}\ \underline{O}\ \underline{W}$ From which I saw a light
        1   59
   late yesterday.

R. $\underline{R}\ \underline{I}\ \underline{C}\ \underline{H}$ $\underline{M}\ \underline{A}\ \underline{N}$ This is what you are,
      19   32
   baby.

S. $\underline{\ }\ \underline{\ }\ \underline{U}\ \underline{D}$ Where I do appreciate your being.
         28 62

T. $\underline{\ }\ \underline{M}\ \underline{\ }\ \underline{\ }\ \underline{I}\ \underline{\ }\ \underline{\ }$ Smash solo single by John.
       38   67

U. $\underline{S}\ \underline{I}\ \underline{\ }\ \underline{L}\ \underline{V}\ \underline{E}\ \underline{R}\ \underline{\ }$ Murderous hammer color.
     12   14

V. $\underline{O}\ \underline{N}\ \underline{I}\ \underline{O}\ \underline{N}\ \underline{\ }$ It's made of glass.
           75 70

W. $\underline{N}\ \underline{A}\ \underline{N}\ \underline{C}\ \underline{Y}$ Her man is Dan.
      39   4

X. $\underline{B}\ \underline{O}\ \underline{N}\ \underline{G}\ \underline{T}\ \underline{T}\ \underline{I}$ Played television director
     51   18
   and mad scientist roles.

86

Y. $\underset{76}{T}\underset{}{R}\underset{6}{U}\underset{}{F}\underset{24}{F}\underset{}{L}\underset{}{E}$ "Savoy _____."

Z. $\underset{29}{A}\underset{77}{B}\underset{53}{B}\underset{}{E}\underset{}{Y}$ $\underset{61}{R}\underset{}{O}\underset{9}{A}\underset{}{D}$ Where Paul walked barefoot.

AA. $\underset{26}{R}\underset{}{I}\underset{}{N}\underset{}{G}\underset{33}{O}$ Beatle with song titled in his honor.

BB. $\underset{56}{R}\underset{}{I}\underset{25}{T}\underset{}{A}$ The well-known lovely maid.

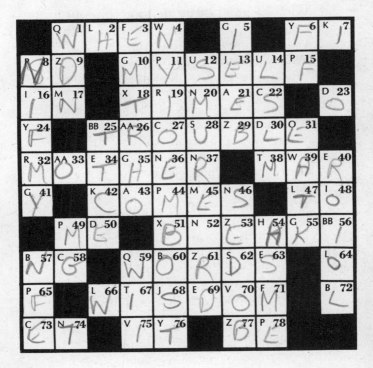

After the Breakup

Although the dream is over, the Beatle melody lingers on. United they changed the world; divided they just keep rolling along. Have you been paying attention?

1. Who was the first Beatle to go on tour in the post-Beatle era?

2. Who was the first to tour America?

3. What was Ringo's first hit single as a solo?

4. Who managed George, Ringo, and John after the breakup?

5. What was the name of John's band on his album, "Sometime in New York City"?

6. What was the basis of the deportation proceeding against John?

7. George named his new label
   A. Mahatma
   B. Weeping Guitar
   C. Black Pony
   D. Dark Horse

8. A photo of which Beatle other than George appears on the inside cover of George's album, "Living in the Material World"?

9. Match the post-split album to the Beatle who recorded it:

A. "Imagine"   John
B. "Ram"   Paul
C. "Sentimental Journey"   George
D. "All Things Must Pass" Ringo

10. (Essay question) Why did the Beatles break up? (Answer in 521 words.)

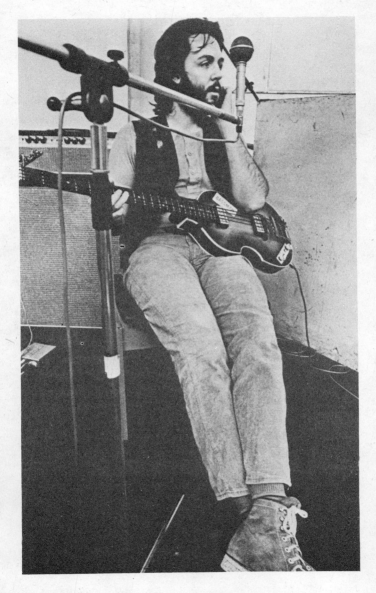

The Connoisseur's Quiz

There are questions here that are so tough even the Beatles themselves couldn't answer them. Here are the scoring rules for the book's toughest test:

0 to 4 correct: I'M A LOSER
5 to 9 correct: I SHOULD HAVE KNOWN BETTER
10 to 14 correct: I FEEL FINE
15 or more correct:If you do this well, you could have written this book, in which case you'd be a PAPER-BACK WRITER.

1. Which American college produced *two* Beatlewives?

2. What was the Beatles' first single in England?

3. Which Conservative Prime Minister is mentioned in TAXMAN?

4. What is the name of the mad scientist's yacht in the movie *Help!*?

5. In what song on the album "A Hard Day's Night" does Paul's voice crack?

6. "Scrambled Egg" was the working title for which Beatlehit?

7. Who designed the Apple label?

8. What kind of apple is on the label?

9. John and Paul wrote WORLD WITHOUT LOVE and NOBODY I KNOW for a British duo named _____

10. How long is the final note of A DAY IN THE LIFE?

11. In which Beatlehit can the listener hear a Beatle say what sounds like "I'm very bored" during the fade? ·

12. Almost everyone knows the Beatles' first introduction to the States was on the Ed Sullivan TV show, but where was their first live American concert?

13. Before George joined the Quarrymen he had his own group. What was its name?

14. What was the first Beatle single on Apple?

15. In what non-Beatle song is it said that "The Beatles' new record's a gas?"

16. Where did John and Paul meet?

17. What was Paul's working title for HEY JUDE?

18. On what two labels did THANK YOU GIRL appear?

19. What is the "butcher cover album?"

20. The Rolling Stones recorded only one Lennon-McCartney tune. What was it?

21. Of the following periodicals, which did George read in *Help!*?

    A. *National Enquirer*
    B. *Queen*
    C. *Wall Street Journal*
    D. *Rolling Stone*
    E. *Queensday*

22. Which line from TELL ME WHY is sung in falsetto?

23. Name Brian Epstein's mother.

24. Where and when was the Beatles' last live concert?

25. Who is Dr. Winston O'Boogie?

THE ANSWERS BEGIN HERE

(According to the Lyrics, Answers)

1. Edison, majoring in medicine. (MAXWELL'S SILVER HAMMER)
2. *Yes, I'm certain that it happens all the time.* (A LITTLE HELP FROM MY FRIENDS)
3. I'VE JUST SEEN A FACE.
4. *I was lonely without her.*
5. B.O.A.C. (BACK IN THE U.S.S.R.)
6. *He blew his mind out in a car.*
7. *Tomorrow I'll miss you.* (ALL MY LOVING)
8. Count them out.
9. Because money can't buy them love. (Everybody tells them so.) (CAN'T BUY ME LOVE)
10. *I got to get a belly full of wine.*
11. No one.
12. *It's a love that had no past.*
13. B.
14. *With a wave of her hand.*
15. *That her baby buys her things, you know. He buys her diamond rings, you know.*
16. Long, cold, lonely.
17. *So far away.*
18. They'll feel okay.
19. All right.
20. Like they've never been born.
21. C. (WE CAN WORK IT OUT)
22. She puts them down.
23. One-night stands.
24. Because *tomorrow may rain.*
25. You'll be free and you'll be like them.

93

(Girls, Answers)

1. ELEANOR RIGBY.
2. Pam.
3. C. (MAXWELL'S SILVER HAMMER)
4. Rose and Valerie (MAXWELL'S SILVER HAMMER)
5. MAGGIE MAE.
6. Nancy. (ROCKY RACCOON)
7. Mother Mary. (LET IT BE)
8. Vera.
9. C.
10. ANNA.
11. SEXY SADIE.
12. DIZZY MISS LIZZIE.
13. JULIA.
14. Martha. (MARTHA MY DEAR)
15. DEAR PRUDENCE.

(Rhyming Lyrics, Answers)

1. . . . *And I do appreciate you being 'round.* (HELP!)

2. . . . *I don't know, I don't know.* (SOMETHING)

3. . . . *It's driving me mad.* (I WANT YOU)

4. . . . *Beneath this mask I am wearing a frown.* (I'M A LOSER)

5. . . . *I thought I knew you*
   What did I know?

6. . . . *And then I might*
   Never be the lonely one.

7. . . . *I'm so proud to know that she is mine.* (GOOD DAY SUNSHINE)

8. . . . *It is no surprise now,*
   What you see is me.

9. . . . *'Cause YOU LIKE ME TOO MUCH and I like you.*

10. . . . *I wouldn't mind if I knew what I was missin'.* (YOU WON'T SEE ME)

(You've Got to Hide Your Love Away, Answers)

1. PERUVIAN PIED PIPER: "WHEN **I FIFE LL**AMAS COME RUNNING."

2. JOHN'S A REAL CO**MIC. HELL, E**VEN PAUL SAYS SO.

3. WERE T**HEY JUDE**O-CHRISTIAN ETHICS OR HINDU MORES?

4. IF YOU MAKE THE MAHARISHI AN OME**LET IT BE**TTER NOT BE A WESTERN.

5. ORIENTAL WOODSMAN'S PROVERB: "SHARP AX, ONE CHOP; BLUN**T AX, MAN**Y CHOPS."

("Yesterday," Answers)

1. It's what the fans in Liverpool chanted when Ringo first took the place of Pete Best, the previous Beatle drummerboy.

2. Quarrymen, Moondogs, Silver Beatles. (All groups in the evolutionary chain that led to the Beatles.)

3. B.

4. John and Paul, when they tried to make it as a duo.

5. A pre-fame Beatle; he died of a brain hemorrhage.

6. Decca.

7. False. (He caught the other Beatles' attention while he was drumming with another group.)

8. Hamburg. (All clubs where the Beatles paid their dues early on.)

9. Singer Tony Sheridan. (On that album alone they were billed as the Beat Boys.)

10. MY BONNIE. (Several requests for this single were made at Epstein's record store; this turned him on to the group.)

(John, Answers)

1. B.
2. Fred.
3. His Aunt Mimi.
4. Winston. (For Churchill, another famous Englishman.)
5. John's son.
6. He doesn't have one. (Sorry.)
7. C.
8. False. (She was first.)
9. True.
10. All of them.

(Paul, Answers)

1. C.
2. False. (It was John and Yoko who slumbered for peace.)
3. Martha.
4. Paul's brother, who has his own singing career.
5. True.
6. Jane Asher, sister of Peter of Peter and Gordon.
7. Africa. (Lagos, Nigeria, to be precise.)
8. It's the location of Paul's farm.
9. Paul. (His full name is James Paul McCartney.)
10. All of them.

(George, Answers)

1. Jelly babies (a tasty anthropomorphic candy not indigenous to the Colonies).
2. True.
3. Gently. (WHILE MY GUITAR GENTLY WEEPS)
4. Ravi Shankar, the sultan of the sitar.
5. Harold and Louise Harrison.
6. A groupie who hangs out at the doorstep of the Apple Records offices in London, as described in George's song, APPLE SCRUFFS.
7. Brown.
8. George's brothers.
9. False. (John said it.)
10. All of them.

(Ringo, Answers)

1. Richard Starkey.
2. The section of Liverpool in which Ringo was reared.
3. True.
4. 1962.
5. Ringo's sons.
6. "I love him, especially his poems."
7. "Because I can't fit them all through my nose."
8. His tonsils.
9. False, but he does have a gray streak.
10. None of them. (Aha!)

("I've Just Seen a Face," Answers)

1. Paul
2. John
3. Ringo
4. George
5. George
6. John
7. Paul
8. Ringo

(Silly Syllables, Answers)

1. DRIVE MY CAR
2. HELLO, GOODBYE
3. HEY JUDE
4. GIRL
5. ALL TOGETHER NOW
6. FROM ME TO YOU
7. BOYS
8. BABY IT'S YOU
9. I AM THE WALRUS
10. HAPPINESS IS A WARM GUN
(Extra credit question) D.

(Flip Sides, Answers)

1. HELP/I'M DOWN
2. TICKET TO RIDE/YES IT IS
3. PAPERBACK WRITER/RAIN
4. GET BACK/DON'T LET ME DOWN
5. YELLOW SUBMARINE/THINGUMYBOB
6. LET IT BE/YOU KNOW MY NAME (LOOK UP MY NUMBER)
7. HELLO, GOODBYE/I AM THE WALRUS
8. I WANT TO HOLD YOUR HAND/I SAW HER STANDING THERE
9. WE CAN WORK IT OUT/DAY TRIPPER
10. HEY JUDE/REVOLUTION

1. The Ukraine; Moscow. (And girls who know how to cook come from Vilna—but that's not in the song.)
2. *Holland or France.*
3. The Seine. (THE BALLAD OF JOHN AND YOKO)
4. *In my ears and in my eyes.* (According to the map, it's in Liverpool.)
5. Bishopsgate. (BEING FOR THE BENEFIT OF MR. KITE)
6. *Somewhere in the black mountain hills of Dakota.*
7. *North of England way.*
8. To your door.
9. The Isle of Wight.
10. D.
11. E. (Strawberry Fields, incidentally, was a Salvation Army girls' hostel that John used to visit for the annual summer garden party.)
12. Their mind. (THERE'S A PLACE)
13. Tuscon, Ariz.; California's. (GET BACK)
14. To where he once belonged.
15. Nowhere land.

(What Do You Know?, Answers)

1. *The sun going down and the world spinning 'round.*

2. They will lose their minds and won't be able to go on.

3. I NEED YOU.

4. A.

5. LET IT BE.

6. *Oh so many ways.*

7. Saturday.

8. *I will follow you and bring you back where you belong.*

9. I don't know. (HELLO, GOODBYE)

10. E. (THE BALLAD OF JOHN AND YOKO) (Subtract five points if you said they ate a Hostess cupcake.)

11. She's going to change her mind, the Beatles will take her out instead, and, undoubtedly, YOU'RE GOING TO LOSE THAT GIRL.

12. Dirty.

13. *Photographs of every head he's had the pleasure to know.*

14. Carve her number on their wall.

15. Gideon's *Bible.*

16. B. (TICKET TO RIDE)

17. Why you cried and why you lied to them.

18. *Wednesday morning at 5 o'clock.*

19. You can't talk to that boy again.

20. Plasticene porters, marshmallow pies, looking glass ties, cellophane flowers, marmalade skies, newspaper taxis, tangerine trees.

(Which Came First?, Answers)

1. "Beatles '65."
2. Paul.
3. The Beatles and LSD.
4. "A Hard Day's Night."
5. Ringo. (Ringo, b. 7/7/40; John, b. 10/9/40.)
6. NOWHERE MAN.
7. *Help!*
8. "The Beatles are more popular than Jesus."
9. Neither—they were released together on the same single.
10. John's marriage to Cynthia.
11. LADY MADONNA.
12. *I get by with a little. . . .*

ORIGINAL MOTION PICTURE SOUNDTRACK

HELP! · THE NIGHT BEFORE · YOU'VE GOT TO HIDE YOUR LOVE AWAY · I NEED YOU
ANOTHER GIRL · TICKET TO RIDE · YOU'RE GONNA LOSE THAT GIRL
And Exclusive Instrumental Music From the Picture's Soundtrack

(Numerology, Answers)

1. *She was just seventeen—you know what I mean.* (I SAW HER STANDING THERE)
2. Seven.
3. Twice.
4. EIGHT DAYS A WEEK.
5. *. . . All good children go to heaven.* (YOU NEVER GIVE ME YOUR MONEY)
6. Ten.
7. *A thousand pages, give or take a few.*
8. *Four thousand.* (A DAY IN THE LIFE)
9. Fifteen. (SHE CAME IN THROUGH THE BATHROOM WINDOW)
10. *One and one and one is three.*

(Analogies, Answers)

1. Liverpudlian. (Term for resident.)
2. The Maharishi. (Song inspiration.)
3. COME TOGETHER. (Flip side.)
4. Algernon. (Assistant, the film *"Help!"*)
5. Harrisongs Ltd. (Song publishing company.)
6. "A Hard Day's Night." (Song and its album.)
7. Paul. (Composer.)
8. "Meet the Beatles." (First album on label.)
9. ELEANOR RIGBY. (Source of quote.)
10. PENNY LANE. (Territory.)

("I Saw a Film Today, Oh Boy," Answers)

1. A.

2. The inhabitants of Pepperland and the Blue Meanies.

3. Nassau (Bahamas) and the Austrian Alps.

4. *Let It Be.*

5. "I bet you're sorry you won."

6. C.

7. Wilfred Brambell.

8. Clang.

9. The Bonzo Dog Band.

10. The conductor of the Lonely Hearts Club Band in *Yellow Submarine.*

11. The incredible shrinking Paul.

12. EIGHT ARMS TO HOLD YOU.

13. Time, Music, Science, Monsters, Consumer Products, Nowhere, Green Phrenology, Holes.

14. On the roof of Apple headquarters.

15. The Chief Blue Meanie, or "Your Blueness."

16. The "Ode to Joy" from Beethoven's *Ninth Symphony.*

17. *Anatomy of a Murder.*

18. *Yellow Submarine.*

19. By setting off an alarm clock over the telephone.

20. Norm and Shake.

21. Director of *Let It Be.*

22. Sgt. Pepper's Lonely Hearts Club Band.

23. The gallant Ringo had spread his coat over an open manhole.

24. A. (If the answer had been D how could it be called "the underwear scene"?)

25. A. George
    B. Ringo
    C. John
    D. Paul

(Multiple Choice, Answers)

1. B. (SGT. PEPPER'S LONELY HEARTS CLUB BAND)
2. E.
3. D. (BEING FOR THE BENEFIT OF MR. KITE)
4. D.
5. C.
6. D.
7. C.
8. C. (Not only is it not on the album, but there's no such Beatlesong.)
9. C. (A LITTLE HELP FROM MY FRIENDS)
10. E.
11. All but E.
12. D. (SGT. PEPPER'S LONELY HEARTS CLUB BAND)

("With a Little Help from My Friends," Answers)

1. Chuck Berry.
2. TILL THERE WAS YOU.
3. KANSAS CITY.
4. A TASTE OF HONEY.
5. EVERYBODY'S TRYING TO BE MY BABY and HONEY DON'T, from "Beatles '65."
6. Little Richard.
7. WORDS OF LOVE.
8. YOU REALLY GOT A HOLD ON ME.
9. TWIST AND SHOUT.
10. Larry Williams.

(True or False, Answers)

1. True.
2. True—7:11, to be exact.
3. False.
4. True.
5. True.
6. True.
7. True.
8. False—he went first class.
9. False.
10. False—it's 90 minutes.

(Anatomy of the Beatles, Answers)

1. *I've got arms that long to hold you and keep you by my side,*
       I've got lips that long to kiss you and keep you satisfied.
2. C.
3. Broken wings, sunken eyes.
4. *He got hair down to his knee; monkey finger and joo joo eyeball.*
5. *Ten-bob note.* (MEAN MR. MUSTARD)

(Who Sang Lead?, Answers)

1. A. John, B. George, C. Ringo
2. A. Paul, B. John, C. Ringo
3. A. George, B. John, C. Paul
4. A. John and Paul, B. Paul, C. George
5. A. John, B. Paul, C. George

("Say the Word," Answers)

1. Go.
2. MISERY.
3. Blue.
4. Tenderly.
5. Nothing.
6. You.
7. You.
8. You. (TILL THERE WAS YOU)
9. Glad.
10. C.
11. Nobody.
12. Blue. (Surprise!)

("Do You Want to Know a Secret?", Answers)

1. Paul.
2. An American merchandising arm of the Beatle empire.
3. John.
4. He collaborated on the screenplay of *Yellow Submarine*.
5. A. Mal Evans
   B. Neil Aspinall
   C. Dick James
   D. Richard Lester
   E. Derek Taylor
   F. Brian Epstein
6. "Why, none other than Billy Preston!"
7. Ltd.
8. Jim McCartney, Paul's dad.
9. They were all managed, at the same time, by Brian Epstein.
10. No. 3 Savile Row.

(Song Fragments, Answers)

1. I AM THE WALRUS.
2. HAPPINESS IS A WARM GUN.
3. LOVELY RITA.
4. BEING FOR THE BENEFIT OF MR. KITE.
5. REVOLUTION.
6. OLD BROWN SHOE.
7. LADY MADONNA.
8. GOOD DAY SUNSHINE.
9. SHE CAME IN THROUGH THE BATHROOM WINDOW.
10. YELLOW SUBMARINE.

(Song Beginnings, Answers)

1. COME AND GET IT.
2. ALL YOU NEED IS LOVE.
3. DO YOU WANT TO KNOW A SECRET?
4. HAPPINESS IS A WARM GUN.
5. HERE, THERE AND EVERYWHERE.
6. DIG IT.
7. EVERYBODY'S GOT SOMETHING TO HIDE EXCEPT ME AND MY MONKEY.
8. GOLDEN SLUMBERS.
9. GLASS ONION.
10. GOOD MORNING, GOOD MORNING.

(Song Endings, Answers)

1. TICKET TO RIDE.
2. P.S. I LOVE YOU.
3. OB-LA-DI, OB-LA-DA.
4. PIGGIES.
5. OH! DARLING.
6. I WANT TO TELL YOU.
7. RUN FOR YOUR LIFE.
8. MISERY.
9. SHE LOVES YOU.
10. LITTLE CHILD

(Extra credit question) An ultrasonic whistle, inaudible to humans. The ending was planned by Paul "as a message for Martha [his Shetland sheepdog] and for all other dogs in the world."

112

(Name That Tune, Answers)

1. I WANT TO HOLD YOUR HAND.
2. ...YOUR MOTHER SHOULD KNOW.
3. TAXMAN.
4. HOLD ME TIGHT.
5. NOT A SECOND TIME.
6. YOU NEVER GIVE ME YOUR MONEY.
7. I'M SO HAPPY JUST TO DANCE WITH YOU.
8. ...AND YOUR BIRD CAN SING.
9. WHAT GOES ON.
10. P.S. I LOVE YOU.
11. IT WON'T BE LONG.
12. DON'T BOTHER ME.
13. THE NIGHT BEFORE.
14. THINK FOR YOURSELF.
15. THINGS WE SAID TODAY.

(Beatle Grab Bag, Answers)

1. John
2. It was announced that they were to be made Members of the Order of the British Empire.
3. THIS BIRD HAS FLOWN.
4. YESTERDAY.
5. C.
6. The tabla.
7. A DAY IN THE LIFE; *I'd love to turn you on.*
8. The Royal Family. (John made the uppity remark at a command performance in 1963.)
9. All sat at the feet of the Maharishi Mahesh Yogi.
10. A string quartet.
11. They're both clean.
12. Creme tangerine, ginger sling, pineapple heart, coffee dessert.

(What's Their Line?, Answers)

1. *Meter maid.*
2. She's *the singer in a band.*
3. He *works for the Daily Mail.*
4. He's *the eggman.*
5. They sell *poppies from a tray.*

("Well Here's Another Clue for You," Answers)

1. Three Beatles sport red flowers; Paul's is ominously black.
2. *I buried Paul.*
3. Since Paul alone wore no hat, it was theorized that he would catch a severe cold leading to "fatal complications."
4. C.
5. The flowers, it was said, were in the shape of Paul's bass guitar, which was thereby symbolically buried along with him.
6. The license read "28IF," indicating that Paul would have been 28 years old IF he had been alive when the album was released.
7. Jesus.
8. The undertaker.
9. The gravedigger.
10. Paul had a look-alike.

(Complete the Lyric, Answers)

1. . . . *Step right this way.*

2. . . . *And I'll try not to sing out of key.* (A LIT-TLE HELP FROM MY FRIENDS)

3. . . . *Can I bring my friend to tea?* (ALL TOGETHER NOW)

4. . . . *I love you.* (ALL TOGETHER NOW)

5. . . . *So Ple-e-e-ease LOVE ME DO.*

6. . . . *And maybe I'll love you.*

7. . . . *Love is you.*

8. . . . *They slither while they pass, they slip away ACROSS THE UNIVERSE.*

9. . . . *'Cause I've just lost the only girl I had.* (I'LL CRY INSTEAD)

10. . . . *I'M ONLY SLEEPING.*

11. . . . *Love to hear you say that love is love.* (THINGS WE SAID TODAY)

12. . . . *I CALL YOUR NAME.*

13. . . . *Would you lock the door?* (WHEN I'M SIXTY-FOUR)

14. . . . *Whisper in your ear the words you long to hear and I'll be kissing you.*

15. . . . *Sont les mots qui vont tres bien ensemble, tres bien ensemble.*

Puzzle 1:

```
X R E R D A E D Y L L A E R S I L U A P
C K C A B E B L L I N M Y L I F E F B Y
B O E C F K E B R M W T U K Y O B D A B
D M N Y S X O D E D I F I F E L L R I G
E M O M T Y R E K O L T I G I D S B N I
R G O E S H E S A W O M A N N A T S N R
I I N V N Z P A K N P S M O N E Y M D R
T B R I Q B L L Z T A R T T B L E E I O
O M O R L F M A E A I U H A F U S M A N
S I F D P P N F N H R A E S T V I I S A
M R W H R E B T I T E L W E W D T N E E
I D H J S I V D C O P B A C O G I E H L
M E A B U N U N E D P L L O O E S E S E
A I T S N G I L U T I A R N F I H D D D
L N G N K O R A I N R C U D U P L Y I U
O E O A I M W K H A T K S T S Y P O A J
S H E M N L E O U C Y B V I Z E R U S Y
E A S X G L Y W T U A I W M Z N T L E E
R N O A N W Z R H O D R X E Y O Y D H H
A D N T H G I N S Y A D D R A H A D S T
```

Puzzle 2:

```
E I Z Z I L S S I M A B E E T H O V E N
T B S C H U C K R E P P E P T G S L H R
H G I E L A R R E T L A W R I S E G O E
G Z B E I Z N E K C M R E H T A F C N D
I U M O L L Y M T Z H M A O N H K H I O
L K L Q D L L I G A M G I O U Y O K O M
N I L A E E L R U N V F R T V J U L I A
O A N N O D A M D N O M S E D G L F J T
O W M R P O S T M A N E J S P I I E K T
M R A R E V K S V L U A P A B F Y D L E
R T R Y T E G G M A N I M W W E I C D R
M O T H E R M A R Y U R O E X D K A U O
A L H O R I T A W N M L E R R C V O M L
X M A F B S L R I U A L K R A E X L N G
W B T T R P N O S G L J O N E S H M O N
E E Z W O W R T N E B B L Q Y B L W P I
L R N P W A A U H Y E C N E D U R P O K
L O F T N R B C X R C D M P Z Y C N A N
O P B S D C I L T E I D A S Y X E S Q U
E T I K R M O J O J B I N O A E D U J S
```

117

(Mixed Beatles, Answers)

1. All appear in the movie *Yellow Submarine.*
2. C.
3. Allen B. Klein, one-time manager of three-fourths of the Beatles.
4. A.
5. 16 (6 for John, 6 for George, 4 for Paul—Ringo was stringless).
6. FLYING was written by all four Beatles.
7. D.
8. The movie *Help!*
9. SHE LOVES YOU.
10. *Honey Pie, Honey Pie, Honey Pie, Honey Pie, Honey Pie, Honey Pie, Honey Pie, Honey Pie, I love you, Honey Pie.*
11. Sitar.
12. "The Beatles' Second Album."

(Information Please, Answers)

1. You *should be sleeping like a log.* (A HARD DAY'S NIGHT)

2. *Give me mo', hey hey hey, give me mo'.*

3. *I know you never even try, girl.*

4. E.

5. Sir Walter Raleigh.

6. A.

7. Lemonade. (RAIN)

8. *I think I'll love you too.* (I'M SO HAPPY JUST TO DANCE WITH YOU)

9. *A love like ours.*

10. *'Bout a week or two.*

11. FIXING A HOLE.

12. LOOK UP MY NUMBER.

13. C. (OB-LA-DI, OB-LA-DA)

14. ANY TIME AT ALL.

15. A silver spoon.

16. Because they're *so sad and lonely.*

17. D. (MOTHER NATURE'S SON)

18. MR. POSTMAN.

19. *Many, many, many times before.*

20. She has the DEVIL IN HER HEART.

21. Their baby.

22. *Working for peanuts.*

23. *Hey, Bungalow Bill—what did you kill, Bungalow Bill?* (THE CONTINUING STORY OF BUNGALOW BILL)

24. The world.

25. B.

(Multiple Choice Revisited, Answers)

1. B.
2. B. (THE BALLAD OF JOHN AND YOKO)
3. C.
4. B.
5. D.
6. D. (I AM THE WALRUS)
7. A. (DR. ROBERT)
8. A.
9. C.
10. A. (BECAUSE)
11. C. (By the way, a wuntoo tree, in case you were wondering, is Lawrence Welk's favorite.)
12. B.

("With Love from Me to You," Answers)

1. A
2. C
3. A
4. B

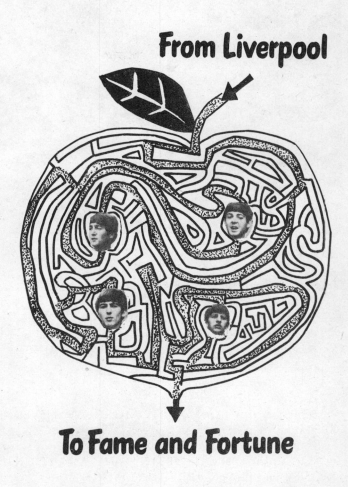

From Liverpool

To Fame and Fortune

(What's Missing?, Answers)

1. *Just holding hands.* (IF I FELL)
2. *Break my heart.*
3. *Miss you.* (ALL MY LOVING)
4. *Make it better.* (HEY JUDE)
5. *Cried.* (THE LONG AND WINDING ROAD)
6. *Inverted.*
7. *Om.* (ACROSS THE UNIVERSE)
8. *Trend.* (PENNY LANE)
9. *Float downstream.* (TOMORROW NEVER KNOWS)
10. *Father McKenzie.* (ELEANOR RIGBY)
11. *Number* (YOU NEVER GIVE ME YOUR MONEY) or *pillow* (CARRY THAT WEIGHT).
12. *The end.*
13. *You and me.*
14. *Trivialities.*

(Beatlecrostic, Answers)

A. LOVE
B. ELEANOR
C. NORTHERN SONGS
D. NO REPLY
E. OCTOPUS'S GARDEN
F. NEMS
G. MARY HOPKINS
H. CARRY
I. CAPITOL
J. ACHES
K. RICHARD
L. THROWS IT AWAY
M. NEVER
N. ELEPHANT'S MEMORY
O. YES
P. HELP FROM MY FRIENDS
Q. A WINDOW
R. RICH MAN
S. 'ROUND
T. IMAGINE
U. SILVER
V. ONION
W. NANCY
X. SPINETTI
Y. TRUFFLE
Z. ABBEY ROAD
AA. RINGO
BB. RITA

(After the Breakup, Answers)

1. Paul.
2. George.
3. IT DON'T COME EASY.
4. Allen B. Klein. (Paul was handled by Lee Eastman, Linda's dad.)
5. Elephant's Memory.
6. He had been arrested for possession of marijuana.
7. D.
8. Ringo.
9. A. John
   B. Paul
   C. Ringo
   D. George
10. The world has not yet recovered from the disintegration of the most important musical group of the 1960s—the Beatles. The sudden cutting of the bonds that linked John, Paul, George, and Ringo stunned millions who had come to think of the brilliant Englishmen as an eternal rainbow in the international musical sky.

Now, years later, the question is still being asked: Why did they split?

It all started with Yoko Ono, a demure, charming girl—or so everyone thought. But shortly after she married John, Yoko began to display a mysterious, hypnotic power apparently acquired in the Orient. As one family friend revealed, "Yoko is a quiet, sweet girl in public, all right. But at home with John it's kvetch, kvetch, kvetch."

"Assert yourself, John," she would nag. "You sing the best, you play the best, and you're the best-looking. Why do you let those leeches butt in on your solos? You could become another Tom Jones.

"You're the star—why don't you take the billing

125

you deserve? Call the group Yoko's Husband and His Three Sidemen.''

Ringo, the sexiest percussionist since John Philip Sousa's star cymbal player, was next to get into the act. He was all in favor of a new name for the quartet, but he had his own idea. Since 1965, of course, the musicians had been members of the prestigious Order of the British Empire, by appointment of the Queen, and Ringo did not take that position lightly. In short order, he had begun to wear a monocle, affected an Etonian accent, and acquired a string of polo ponies.

It was time, he declared, for the whole group to live up to its distinguished honor. The name he proposed was the Liverpool String Trio Plus Percussion.

George also had a suggestion. As all fans well remember, the Beatles spent considerable time one year in the practice of transcendental meditation at the feet of the Maharishi Mahesh Yogi.

While the others went along on the advice of their public relations consultant, like good Beatles, George got carried away. He stopped eating meat and became a rhubarb freak, he took to playing the sitar on mountain tops, and more than once he was seen wandering Carnaby Street mumbling, ''Life is a fountain, life is a fountain.''

With tears in his eyes, George pleaded that the band rename itself the Mahatma Gandhi Memorial Quartet.

To top things off, Paul also wanted to have his tuppence worth. Since his marriage to American-born Linda Eastman, he had begun to acquire a goodly number of Yankee ways. He gave up tea and switched to Dr. Pepper, he traded in his two Rolls-Royces for a Cadillac and a Volkswagen, and he began offering taxi drivers a handful of change say-

ing, "Here—take whatever I owe you. I don't understand your confounded English money."

When the topic of a new name came up, the Americanized Paul had a great inspiration. "I agree it's time for a change," he said. "Let's call ourselves the Mills Brothers."

It was obvious that the Beatles, as individuals, were miles apart. It was all over.

(The Connoisseur's Quiz, Answers)

1. Sarah Lawrence, which claims as alumnae Linda Eastman and Yoko Ono.
2. LOVE ME DO/P.S. I LOVE YOU.
3. Mr. Heath.
4. Sceptre (of America's Cup fame).
5. IF I FELL. (Listen closely.)
6. YESTERDAY.
7. Gene Mahon.
8. Granny Smith.
9. Peter and Gordon.
10. 43 1/2 seconds.
11. STRAWBERRY FIELDS.
12. The Washington Coliseum.
13. The Rebels.
14. HEY JUDE/REVOLUTION.
15. The Temptations' BALL OF CONFUSION.
16. At the Woolton Parish Church, where Paul had come to hear John's group play at a dance.
17. "Hey Jules."
18. Capitol and Vee Jay.
19. "'Yesterday'... and Today," which was first released in a jacket for which the Beatles posed as butchers of babies. The controversial jacket was quickly replaced.
20. I WANNA BE YOUR MAN.
21. C.
22. *Is there anything I can do?*
23. Queenie.
24. Candlestick Park, San Francisco, August 29, 1966.
25. A pseudonym used by John.

128